Cites & Sources

Jane Haig   Gail Raikes   Vicki Sutherland

Georgian College

THOMSON
—★—
NELSON

Australia   Canada   Mexico   Singapore   Spain   United Kingdom   United States

THOMSON

——★——™

NELSON

Cites and Sources

by Jane Haig, Gail Raikes, Vicki Sutherland

Editorial Director and Publisher:
Evelyn Veitch

Executive Editor:
Chris Carson

Marketing Manager:
Cara Yarzab

Senior Developmental Editor:
Rebecca Rea

Managing Production Editor:
Susan Calvert

Production Coordinator:
Helen Jager Locsin

Proofreader:
Edie Franks

Creative Director:
Angela Cluer

Cover Design:
Anne Bradley

Interior Design:
Tara McLellan

Cover Photo:
Katherine Strain

Printer:
Transcontinental Printing Inc.

**National Library of Canada
Cataloguing in Publication Data**

Haig, Jane
   Cites and sources/Jane Haig, Gail
   Raikes, Vicki Sutherland.

Includes index.
ISBN 0-17-640550-X

1. Authorship—Style manuals—
Handbooks, manuals, etc.
2. Bibliographic citations—
Handbooks, manuals, etc.
I. Raikes, Gail   II. Sutherland,
Vicki.   III. Title.   IV. Title: APA
documentation style guide.

PN171.F56H34 2003   C813'.6
C2002-905673-X

Table of Contents

Introduction to APA

The American Psychological Association (APA) style of documentation is commonly recognized as a standard documentation style for colleges, universities, and businesses.

A consistent style of documentation in research papers

Provides *uniformity* to the paper

Allows **readers** to give full *attention* to content

Presents *ideas* in a form and style accepted by and familiar to readers

Acknowledgements

For their contribution to the development of this project, we express our gratitude to Georgian College, particularly to Dr. Bill Gordon, Dean of University and Advanced Studies, and to Katherine Wallis, Director of the Learning Resource Centre.

We also recognize the considerable time and talents contributed by the following at Georgian College:

Editorial Team Gail Lucas, Faculty, Liberal Arts
Marion Ross, Faculty, Liberal Arts
Janice Schulze, Faculty, Student Services

Interior Design Tara McLellan, Graphic Designer, Georgian Graduate

In addition, we acknowledge the contributions of Sula De Stefano, Dale Lovering, Beth Mawhiney, Heather White, and Mary Whittaker.

Finally, we thank the students and faculty at Georgian College who have prompted, challenged, and inspired us.

"It takes too much time, being afraid."

—Pierre Elliott Trudeau, 1919-2000

Getting Started

Getting Started

Once you have selected a topic for research, you need to consult many sources – including books, magazines, journals, newspapers, and online information. To avoid plagiarism, you must document all ideas and direct quotations in your paper using APA style (see **Plagiarism,** p. 4).

Proper documentation requires that you

Acknowledge source references within your paper (in-text citations)

List your *sources* at the end of your paper (*References* list)

Conflict   2
The Value of Understanding Neighbour
Types in Conflict Resolution
Most people live in urban or suburban areas in close proximity to their neighbours; like family, neighbours cannot always be chosen. Additionally, each person has a different idea of who makes a desirable neighbour. Some might welcome a friendly, helpful neighbour whom others consider intrusive. Most likely, everyone will experience neighbourhood conflict at some time since individuals have their own peculiar habits and levels of tolerance. **Conflict is a perceived incompatibility of actions, goals or ideas (Myers, 1998)** and can be especially difficult when the neighbourhood's conventions are openly defied. When people know their . . .

some time since individuals have their own peculiar habits and levels of tolerance. **Conflict is a perceived incompatibility of actions, goals or ideas (Myers, 1998)** and can be especially difficult when the neighbourhood's conventions are openly...

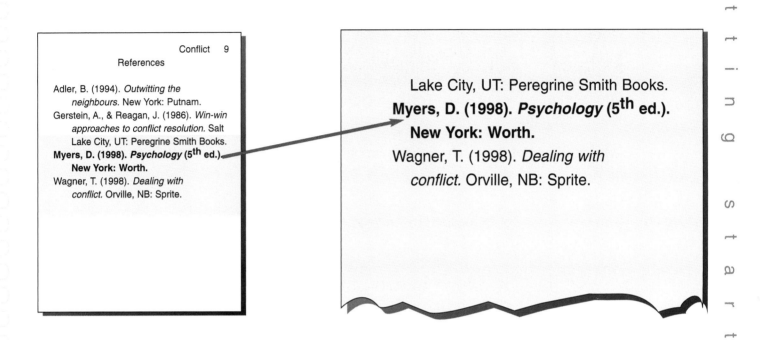

Research

Your research begins with evaluating print and electronic resources to determine the most useful sources of information for your report or paper. Consider the following criteria.

Accuracy: Is the information contained in the document both relevant and accurate? Check the publisher/producer for credibility. For example, a government publication such as *Statistics Canada* can be considered reliable. A web site developed by someone interested in promoting a particular point of view or product using questionable statistics may not be as reliable.

Content: Is there enough detailed information on the topic? Is the information at an appropriate level for the topic?

Authority: Who is responsible for the information? Is the producer/publisher the same as the author? Are credentials listed? Is there an advertiser/sponsor relationship?

Objectivity: Is the information biased? Is the producer actually an advertiser promoting a product? If the resource is a web site, check the domain name for clues to ownership.

Currency: Is the information up-to-date and/or relevant? If the information is from a web site, when was it last updated?

Taking Notes

Research involves taking notes in which you summarize, paraphrase, and directly quote information from your reference sources. Be sure to include all of the information necessary to correctly document your sources when it comes time to write your paper.

While taking notes, clearly distinguish between paraphrased material and direct quotations, and always include

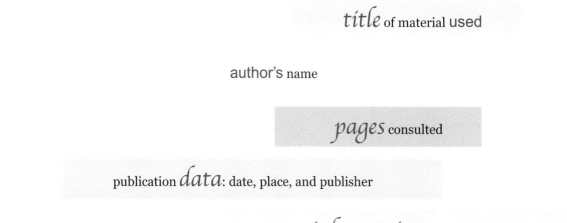

title of material used

author's name

pages consulted

publication *data*: date, place, and publisher

access *information* for electronic materials

Plagiarism

Plagiarism is the act of presenting someone else's words or ideas as your own – and is a **serious academic offence**. Whether you are quoting directly or putting an idea or fact into your own words, you must cite your source (see **Section 3: Citing Sources**).

Penalties for plagiarism, even if unintentional, may range from a zero on the paper to expulsion from the institution. Protect yourself by scrupulously documenting all your sources.

"If you think education is expensive —
try ignorance."

—*Derek Bok*

2

formatting your paper

formatting your paper

Formatting
Your Paper

Formatting Your Paper

A successful research essay or report must be professionally formatted and presented. First impressions count!

This section presents a sample cover page, essay and report models, and a reference page formatted according to the following guidelines. Consult with your instructor or refer to other documentation manuals for more detailed information on formatting and organizing specific kinds of reports.

Materials and Typeface
Use good-quality 8 1/2" x 11" white paper. Select Times New Roman, 12 point, as the preferred font. All documents should be word-processed and printed using a high-quality printer.

Margins, Spacing and Indentation
Use one-inch (2.54 cm) margins on all sides of the page (top, bottom, right and left). Double-space the entire paper, and indent the first line of each paragraph one tab. Tab indent each line of long quotations (longer than forty words), and double-space the lines of the quotation.

Cover/Title Page
Begin your paper with a cover page. Place a short header (one or two key words from the title of the paper) and, separated by five spaces, the page number flush against the right margin, one-half inch (1.27 cm) from the top of the page. Most instructors need more information on the cover page of an APA-style college paper than that specified in the APA manual. In this case, we suggest you create a cover page similar to the one on page 10. Centre and double-space the text in the upper half of the page. Use upper and lower case letters to type the following: the title of your paper, your name, the name and section of your course, your instructor's name, and the date.

Page Numbers and Headers
Type a short identifying header (one or two key words from the title of the paper) and, separated by five spaces, the page number in the top right corner of every page, beginning with the title page. Number all pages, including the cover page, tables, appendices, and the reference page.

Abstract/Summary
An abstract or summary provides an overview of your paper. It should include your central idea, key points, and any implications or applications discussed in your paper. Consult your instructor for more specific details and requirements.

An abstract or summary immediately follows the title page. Type "Abstract" or "Summary" as the main heading, centred and at the top of the page. Omit the usual paragraph indent. An abstract or summary does not usually exceed one page.

Headings

Headings help to organize the presentation of your research and are required for most reports. Centre first-level headings (major divisions), and use mixed case letters. Left justify and italicize sub-headings; used mixed case. For documents requiring more than two levels of heading, refer to the APA manual.

Visuals

Reports often include visuals to clarify and summarize research findings. Visuals are used to complement rather than to duplicate text. Tables, for example, present exact numerical data, arranged in columns and rows. Figures include graphs, charts, maps, illustrations, drawings, and photographs. Tables and figures allow readers to see the overall pattern of results, eliminating the need for lengthy discussion. **Do not, however, include any visuals that you do not clearly introduce and explain in your text.**

Ask your instructor for specific assignment guidelines on placing, labelling, and numbering the pages of your visuals.

Appendix

An appendix is located at the end of a report following the *References* list and contains additional information referred to in the report. For example, you might want to include a copy of a survey form (questionnaire or interview questions) that you used to collect data for your report. Each appendix is labelled Appendix A, B, C, and so on, according to the order it is referred to in the report.

Supplementary Material

Specific kinds of reports may require additional supplementary materials – such as an executive summary, a memo or letter of transmittal, interview transcripts, and so on. Ask your instructor or consult your course textbook as to how to arrange and place these supplementary materials.

Cover Page

Information centred in upper half of page and double-spaced

Header (one or two key words from the title) and, separated by five spaces, the page number

Title in mixed case

Student's name

Course name

Instructor's name

Date

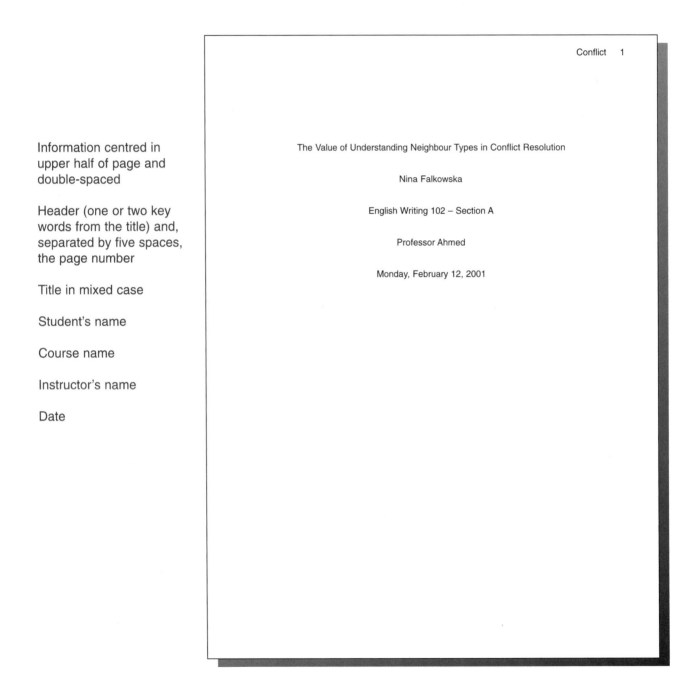

Conflict   1

The Value of Understanding Neighbour Types in Conflict Resolution

Nina Falkowska

English Writing 102 – Section A

Professor Ahmed

Monday, February 12, 2001

Sample Essay

Conflict   2

The Value of Understanding Neighbour Types in Conflict Resolution

Most people live in urban or suburban areas in close proximity to their neighbours; like family, neighbours cannot always be chosen. Additionally, each person has a different idea of who makes a desirable neighbour. For example, having a neighbour who hosts loud parties may be attractive to a fun-loving extrovert, while introverts may prefer quiet neighbours who keep to themselves. Some might welcome a friendly, helpful neighbour whom others consider intrusive. Most likely, everyone will experience neighbourhood conflict at some time since individuals have their own peculiar habits and levels of tolerance. Conflict is a perceived incompatibility of actions, goals or ideas (Myers, 1998) and can be especially difficult when the neighbourhood's conventions are openly defied. When people know their neighbours' types, they can make basic assumptions about how their neighbours will react to conflict and even how their own behaviour may annoy their neighbours. Understanding the habits of the four basic types of neighbours – noisy, fussy, helpful, and gossipy – can lead to resolving neighbourhood conflict.

In *Outwitting the Neighbours*, Adler indicated that "of all the complaints that people have about their neighbours, noise ranks at the top" (1994, p.107). Although individuals can each tolerate different levels of sound, it is the one environmental nuisance that can be measured scientifically. For this reason "nearly every community has a noise ordinance, probably banning noises around 80 dB" (Adler, 1994, p. 107) . . . **[section continues]**.

Include an indentifying header and page number in the top right corner of every page

Centre the title and use mixed case

Double-space between the title and the first line

Tab indent the first line of each paragraph

Double-space all text

Use Times New Roman or a similar font and 12 point type

Leave one-inch (2.54 cm) margins (top, bottom, right and left)

Sample Report

Centre the title and use mixed case

Double-space between the title and first line

Double-space all text

Use Times New Roman or similar font and 12 point type

Centre all main headings

The Greening of the Canadian Hotel Industry

Introduction

In the 1990s, the North American hotel industry began responding to customers' demands for more environmentally friendly service. The need for waste reduction and recycling programs in an industry that routinely disposed of thousands of tonnes of plastics, paper, toiletries, water, and surplus food became increasingly obvious. Following the call to action by groups such as the Green Hotels Association ("Greening," 1998), travelers were encouraged to request "green" hotels for guest stays, meetings, conventions, and family events. Numerous hotels responded by lowering water and energy usage and by reducing solid waste. In Canada, many hotels and resorts have introduced "green" practices and offer a broad range of options for travelers. The purpose of this report is to explore the demand for "greening," current conservation practices, specialized accommodations, and environmental education programs in Canadian hotels and resorts.

Discussion

Today, it is relatively common to find towel and sheet-changing options, low-flow showers and toilets, soap and shampoo dispensers, and room recycling baskets. Frequently, hotel guests across North America now find signs displayed in their bathrooms stating, "Please decide for yourself. A towel on the rack means 'I'll use it several times.' A towel on the floor means 'Please exchange'" (Andrews, 1993, p. 22). Many hotels, however, have taken this movement . . .

[section continues].

Demand for "Greening"

In 1998, the U.S. Travel Data Center estimated that 43 million U.S. travelers were ecologically concerned ("Greening," 1998). In Canada, the situation is much the same. According to a questionnaire distributed in 1992 by Canadian Pacific (CP) Hotels & Resorts, more than 95

Greening   4

percent of their employees viewed the environment as a critical issue, 89 percent wanted to know

more about what they could do to help, and 82 percent agreed to volunteer extra time and effort

to help (Troyer, 1992). Together with government agencies and environmental groups, North

American travelers and employees of the travel industry began agitating for recycling and waste-

reduction programs. The Green Hotels Association distributed "The Meeting Planner's

Questionnaire," urging conference planners to use this as a means of assessing the "greenness"

of a hotel before booking accommodations. The questionnaire covered areas such as "recycling,

purchasing of recycled or recyclable items, food and beverage service, bottle deposits, leftover

food, meeting materials, guestroom amenities, guestroom linens, water and energy conservation"

("Green Hotels," 1997, p. 10). By choosing "green" hotels for meetings and convention sites,

meeting planners began directly influencing the environmental awareness of the hotel industry.

The success of the recent symposium held in Atlanta, Georgia, concerning the management of

the supply and demand of environment-friendly hotels clearly indicates that the greening of hotels

is seen by the industry as simply good for business. In Canada, the number of hotels . . . **[sec-**

tion continues].

Conservation Practices

      Canadian Pacific Hotels was the first major hotel chain in Canada to respond to the con-

sumer demand for conservation. In Phase One of their "Green Partnership" corporate environ-

mental program, CP Hotels placed blue recycling boxes in every one of its hotel rooms, made 90

percent of all used soap available to local charities, recycled 86 percent of all paper used in CP

Hotels into paper that met or exceeded the Canadian Environmental Choice Standards, and

reduced paper consumption by 20 percent in 80 percent of all CP Hotel properties (Jacquette,

1998). CP has also published *The CPH & R Green Partnership Guide* (1992), a handbook

---

Place the page number in the top corner

Leave one-inch (2.54 cm) margins (top, bottom, right and left)

Italicize and left justify sub-headings; use upper and lower (mixed) case

offering practical advice to other hotels, institutions and restaurants on how to create an

environmentally-friendly setting. CP Hotels' initiative was met by . . . **[section continues].**

Specialized Accommodations

While approximately 30 percent of all hotels in Canada today provide recycling bins, refillable

pump dispensers for amenities, low-flow showerheads, faucet aerators and toilets, and energy-sav-

ing lighting and heating systems, many hotels are moving toward providing more comfortable envi-

ronments for allergy and health-conscious customers as well. Steve Belmonte, President and CEO

of Ramada Franchise Systems, noted that particular attention to "food-allergy safe" practices in the

preparation and service of food and beverages in hotels is absolutely necessary to ensure not only

the comfort but also the safety of hotel guests (Marshall, 1995). . . **[section continues].**

Environmental Education Programs

Phase Two of CP Hotels' corporate environmental program is intended to move beyond the

basics of recycling and energy conservation. As Leslee Jaquette (1998) notes, according to

Environmental Affairs Supervisor, Belinda Dusbaba, CP Hotels wants to "'identify best practices,

formalize corporate environmental practices and motivate employees to continue to make positive

changes at each of our 26 properties'" (p. 32). The focus on incentive programs for employees is

perhaps the most innovative . . . **[section continues].**

Conclusion

This examination of the "greening" of the Canadian hotel industry reveals both the success of

current environmentally friendly practices and educational programs – and the need for increased

industry incentives. While several hotels and lodging facilities have . . . **[section continues].**

Include an identifying header and page number on every page

Tab indent the first line of each paragraph

Do not start a new page for subsections (e.g., Conclusion)

Sample Reference Page

References

Andrews, J. (1993, November). Don't throw in the towel! *Environment, 35* (9), 22.

Cleaver, J. (1995). Allergy sufferers find peace, no pollen, in eco-friendly room. *Crain's*
Chicago Business, 18 (44), 24-26.

F.L.C. (2000). Hoteliers and corporate travel buyers to promote "green" hotels together.
Cornell Hotel & Restaurant Administration Quarterly, 41 (5), 16.

Green Hotels Association offers Meeting Planner's Questionnaire. (1997, March/April). *Natural*
Life, 10.

Greening your travel experience. (1998, December). *USA Today Magazine, 127*
(2643), 15.

Holland, R. (1999). Company's products purify air, water in hotel rooms. *Boston Business*
Journal, 19 (19), 9.

Jacquette, L. (1998). Canadian Pacific renews environmental initiative. *Hotel & Motel*
Management, 213 (14), 32.

Marshall, A. (1995). Food allergies nothing to sneeze at. *Hotel & Motel Management, 210* (2),
11.

Mulrine, A. (1999, October 18). Room service, send up a yogi: Hotels are introducing a wave
of New Age perks aimed at business travelers. *U.S. News and World Report, 127* (15), 104.

Troyer, W. (1992). *The CPH & R green partnership guide: 12 steps to help create an*
environmentally-friendly setting for our guests, ourselves and our future. Canada:
Canadian Pacific Hotels & Resorts.

Begin a new page for the
list of *References*

Centre the word
"References" at the top of
the page

Place a header and page
number in the top
right corner

List each entry
alphabetically (according
to the first letter of each
entry)

Set the first line of each
entry flush left and indent
subsequent lines

Double space *all* lines

"It is not necessary to change … survival is not mandatory."

–W. Edwards Deming

3

Citing Sources

Citing Sources

You must acknowledge any ideas or facts used to write your paper by citing the author and date of the source consulted. In text-citations

Identify the sources used to compile your *research*

Lead readers to *entries* in the *References* list located at the end of your paper

Two ways to cite

Direct Quotation
directly quoting someone else's words

or

Paraphrasing
putting the author's ideas into your *own* words

Building a Citation

A citation acknowledges the research source you used to emphasize, reinforce, or prove any point you made in your research paper. Research papers that do not cite sources could be liable for plagiarism. You must document your sources!

A citation includes (within brackets) the author's surname and the publication date.

A citation follows an idea or fact taken from a research source.

The period for the sentence is placed after the citation – not before.

Basic author-date
A citation in APA style follows the author-date method.

 Author Date

(Troyer, 1992)

Author, no date

If there is no date available for the citation, the abbreviation **n.d.** is used.

Author	n.d.

(Grieger, n.d.)

Direct Quotation

The citation following a direct quotation must include the page reference.

Author	Date	p. #

(Myers, 1998, p. 58)

Electronic Sources

Often electronic sources do not provide page numbers. In this case, use the paragraph number, if available, preceded by "para." If neither paragraph nor page numbers are available or appropriate, cite the heading of the document to direct your reader to the location of your source material.

Author	Date	para. #

(Statistics Canada, 1999, para. 4)

Author	Date	Section Heading

(Cancer Care Ontario, 2000, Conclusion section)

Using Direct Quotations

Work direct quotations into the grammatical structure and logic of your own sentences. Clearly indicate the relevance of the quoted material to your discussion. Never insert a quotation without an introduction.

Provide the author's name, the publication year, and the page number in an in-text citation directly following the quotation.

Short Quotations

Incorporate a short, direct quotation (fewer than 40 words) directly into the text of your paper and enclose it in double quotation marks.

Certainly, as social-cognitive research has shown, "the best way to predict someone's behavior in a given situation is to observe that person's behavior pattern in similar situations" (Myers, 1998, p. 451).

Note that the period *follows* the citation at the end of a short quotation.

Long Quotations

Set longer quotations (40 words or more) off from the rest of your written text by block indenting the quotation one tab from the left margin. Double-space the entire quotation and do not enclose it in quotation marks.

A soaring increase in immune-related diseases such as rheumetoid arthritis, diabetes, lupus, allergies and asthma has encouraged doctors and scientists to look more seriously at the overcleanliness theory first advanced in 1989 by epidemologist David Strachan:

> The "dirt" theory holds that immune systems learn to cope with the multitude of bacteria in filth and impure water from the moment of birth. The onslaught helps develop sophisticated immune cells, mostly in childhood. Without germs the immunity does not develop. ( )
>
> An infant's immune system will become impaired if it is forced to grow in a sterile environment, says Graham Rook, an immunologist at University College London. John Fraser of the Auckland University School of Medicine says, "There is good scientific reason for believing that the fewer infectious diseases a person meets early in life, the more likely the immune system will be hypersensitive to allergens like pollens and dust mites." (Downey, 1999, p. 50)

Note that the period is placed *before* the in-text citation in a long quotation. Use double quotation marks, as in the example above, to indicate quoted material within your source quotation (quotation within a quotation).

Quotation Within a Quotation

Cite the source from which you are quoting. For example, to reference a quotation by a government official in an article written by Pascal in *The Toronto Star*, cite Pascal as the author.

The Toronto Star reported that new legislation would allow police in Ontario "to seize the assets from suspected organized criminals. As a government source explained, 'If you are the victim of organized crime, say through a credit-card scam or that type of thing, then you would have the option of applying for that money'" (Pascal, 2000, p. A1).

Note the use of double and single quotation marks.

Paraphrasing

Paraphrasing an idea means putting the author's ideas into your own words. When paraphrasing, you must

Introduce the *author's name* as part of your sentence and include only the publication date in the brackets following the paraphrased material (signal phrase).

or

Include the *author's name and the publication date* in the brackets following the paraphrased material (no signal phrase).

Although not required, you should also include the page number when it would help an interested reader locate the relevant passage in a long or complex text.

Paraphrase (signal phrase)

According to Greg Keenan of *The Globe and Mail*, Ford Motor Co. of Canada donated $3 million to St. Clair College in Windsor, Ontario, in an unprecedented effort to address a shortage of skilled autoworkers (2000).

Paraphrase (no signal phrase)

In an unprecedented effort to address a shortage of skilled autoworkers, Ford Motor Co. of Canada donated $3 million to St. Clair College in Windsor, Ontario (Keenan, 2000).

Example of paraphrasing within a report or research paper

In 1998, the U.S. Travel Data Center estimated that 43 million U.S. travellers were ecologically concerned ("Greening," 1998). In Canada, the situation is much the same. According to a questionnaire distributed in 1992 by Canadian Pacific (CP) Hotels & Resorts, more than 95 percent of their employees viewed the environment as a critical issue, 89 percent wanted to know more about what they could do to help, and 82 percent agreed to volunteer extra time and effort to help (Troyer, 1992). . . . **[section continues].**

Canadian Pacific Hotels was the first major hotel chain in Canada to respond to the consumer demand for conservation. In Phase One of their "Green Partnership" corporate environmental program, CP Hotels placed blue recycling boxes in every one of its hotel rooms, made 90 percent of all used soap available to local charities, recycled 86 percent of all paper used in CP Hotels into paper that met or exceeded the Canadian Environmental Choice Standards, and reduced paper consumption by 20 percent in 80 percent of all CP Hotel properties (Jacquette, 1998). CP has also published *The CPH & R Green*.... **[section continues]**.

Note the use of a shortened version of the title for an article with no author, as in ("Greening," 1998), above.

In-Text References to Books and Articles

The rules for capitalizing and italicizing titles in the text or body of your report or essay are different from those you should follow for your citations (bracketed information) and for your reference list entries. When you want to discuss a work in the body of your report, observe the following rules.

In-Text References to Books, Films and Periodicals (Entire Works)

To refer to a book, film, or periodical (an entire magazine or newspaper), capitalize the first letter of each word in the title and italicize the title. Do not capitalize articles ("a" and "an"), prepositions ("in," "at," etc.), or conjunctions ("but, "and," "or") unless they are the first word of a title or follow a colon.

Canadian Pacific Hotels has also published *The CPH & R Green Partnership Guide* (1992), a handbook offering practical advice to other hotels, institutions and restaurants on how to create an environmentally-friendly setting.

In-Text References to Articles and Chapters

To refer to an article or chapter from a book or periodical, capitalize the first letter of each word in the title and place the title in quotation marks.

Leslee Jaquette's article, "Canadian Pacific Renews Environmental Intiative," outlines Phase Two of CP Hotels' corporate environmental program.

"You must do the thing you think you cannot do."

–Eleanor Roosevelt, 1884-1962

using in-text citations

Using In-Text
Citations

Using In-Text Citations

APA format requires the author-date method of citation. Periods, commas, and semicolons are placed outside the citation. The following lists some guidelines and examples.

Articles in Books or Periodicals

1. SINGLE AUTHOR
2. SINGLE AUTHOR (Signal Phrase)
3. MULTIPLE WORKS BY ONE AUTHOR
4. MULTIPLE WORKS BY ONE AUTHOR WITH THE SAME DATE
5. NO AUTHOR
6. TWO AUTHORS
7. THREE TO FIVE AUTHORS
8. SIX OR MORE AUTHORS
9. TWO OR MORE WORKS BY DIFFERENT AUTHORS
10. GROUP OR CORPORATE AUTHOR
11. SPECIFIC PARTS OF A SOURCE
12. WORK DISCUSSED IN A SECONDARY SOURCE
13. QUOTATION WITHIN A QUOTATION
14. CLASSIC WORKS
15. PARTS OF CLASSIC WORKS

Electronic Sources

16. SINGLE AUTHOR
17. NO DATE
18. NO AUTHOR
19. MULTIPLE AUTHORS
20. ENTIRE WEB SITE

Other Publications

21. COMIC STRIP, PHOTOGRAPH, OR ILLUSTRATION
22. DICTIONARY/ENCYCLOPEDIA DEFINITION
23. PERSONAL COMMUNICATION

Articles in Books or Periodicals

Magazines, journals, and newspapers are considered "periodicals." The following examples show how to cite references to ideas and facts from books and/or periodicals.

1. Single Author

Cite the author's surname and the date of publication: (Jaquette, 1998)

Canadian Pacific's (CP) recent move to Phase Two of its corporate environmental program indicates the success of the North American movement towards the "greening" of hotels (Jaquette, 1998).

2. Single Author (Signal Phrase)
If you indicate the author's name in the body of your sentence, cite only the date of publication: (1998)

Canadian Pacific's (CP) recent move to Phase Two of its corporate environmental program, as reported in Leslee Jaquette's article, indicates the success of the North American movement towards the "greening" of hotels (1998).

3. Multiple Works by One Author
List multiple works by one author within a single set of brackets in chronological order: (Frye, 1963, 1967, 1988, 1990).

His numerous publications on education reflect his lifelong commitment to the value of teaching literature (Frye, 1963, 1967, 1988, 1990).

4. Multiple Works by One Author With the Same Date
Use suffixes (a, b, c, and so on) to identify multiple works by one author published in the same year.

That year he published several studies on education as well as literary criticism (Frye, 1963a, 1963b, 1963c).

In the *References* list, order these works alphabetically by title.

5. No Author
Use one or two key words from the title followed by the year. Use double quotation marks around the title of an article or chapter; italicize the title of a periodical, book, brochure or report. For example, for an article titled "Aspirin Causes Bleeding," use the following: ("Aspirin," 2000)

Researchers have discovered that long-term use of Aspirin to prevent heart problems can increase the risk of gastrointestinal bleeding ("Aspirin," 2000).

6. Two Authors
Cite both authors' surnames joined by an "&": (Anderson & Dill, 2000)

A recent major study conducted by the Psychology Department at the University of Missouri-Columbia showed that real-life violent video game play increases aggressive behaviour and delinquency (Anderson & Dill, 2000).

7. Three to Five Authors

Cite all the authors' surnames in the first reference; for subsequent references include only the surname of the first author followed by "et al." and the year: (Holowaty, Marrett, Parkes, & Fehringer, 1998)

Colorectal cancer was the second most common cause of cancer death for Ontario residents from 1992-1996 (Holowaty, Marrett, Parkes, & Fehringer, 1998).

Subsequent references: (Holowaty, et al., 1998)

8. Six or More Authors

Cite only the surname of the first author followed by "et al." and the year for the first and subsequent references: (Murless, et al., 2001)

In the *References* list, however, include the initials and surnames of each author.

9. Two or More Works by Different Authors

To cite several studies by different authors, cite the authors' names in alphabetical order inside one set of brackets. Separate the citations by semicolons: (Cleaver, 1995; Holland, 1999; Marshall, 1995)

Numerous articles (Cleaver, 1995; Holland, 1999; Marshall, 1995) suggest that the "green" movement of the hotel industry has gone beyond the "reduce, re-use, recycle" environmental golden rule.

10. Group or Corporate Author

Groups as authors include corporations, businesses, associations, government agencies, and study groups.

Cite the name of the group in the first reference: (Canadian Council of Ministers of the Environment [CCME], 1999)

Subsequent references may be abbreviated as indicated in the initial citation: (CCME, 1999)

Government guidelines exist to regulate and monitor treatment processes for drinking water (CCME, 1999).

11. Specific Parts of a Source

To cite a part of a work, indicate the chapter, figure, table, or equation: (Klein, 2000, chap. 17)

This section of her study provides an excellent discussion of recent student and community action against the brand bullies (Klein, 2000, chap. 17).

12. Work Discussed in a Secondary Source

Cite the source in which you found the information – not the original work. For example, to refer to an idea or fact from a book written by Katz discussed in an article written by Jones, cite Jones, not Katz as your source: (Jones, 2000, p. 89)

As Jones discusses, Katz's study indicated that, historically, ideals of beauty have had a negative impact on women's health (Jones, 2000).

In Katz's study of teenaged girls' eating disorders he concluded that "myths of femininity largely function to disable women's health and well-being" (as cited in Jones, 2000, p. 89).

Note the use of "as cited in" in the example above of a direct quotation taken from another source.

13. Quotation Within a Quotation

Use single quotation marks within double quotation marks to indicate material quoted in a source text (quotation within a quotation). Cite the source in which you found the information – not the original work.

The Toronto Star reported that new legislation would allow police in Ontario "to seize the assets from suspected organized criminals. As a government source explains, 'If you are the victim of organized crime, say through a credit-card scam or that type of thing, then you would have the option of applying for that money'" (Pascal, 2000, p. A1).

14. Classic Works

When citing old works, cite both the original publication date and the date of your version: (Shelley, 1818/2000)

For very old works for which the date of publication is unavailable, cite the year of the translation you used, preceded by "trans." or the year of the version you used followed by "version": (Plato, trans. 1955)

15. Parts of Classic Works

Refer to parts of major classical works (Greek and Roman works, the Bible, Shakespeare, and so on) in the text of your paper by part (e.g., books, chapters, verses, lines, cantos). For example, following a quotation of lines 129 and 130 in Act 1, Scene 2 of William Shakespeare's *Hamlet*, cite the following: (1.2.129-130)

Electronic Sources

Use the same format to cite electronic sources as you would to cite a print source (see **Building a Citation**, p. 18). If an electronic document does not indicate the name of the author(s), place in the author position either a shortened version of the title or the name of the organization that published the document. Readers will know to look in the *References* page under the term chosen in place of the author.

16. Single Author

Cite the author's surname and the date of publication or update or the date of retrieval: (Cornell, 2002)

In order to maximize your return when selling a business, you should consider

delaying any capital and discretionary expenses (Cornell, 2002).

17. No Date

Write "n.d." if there is no date of publication: (Grieger, n.d.)

Caffeine intake is considered moderate at 200–300 mg per day, or 3 cups of coffee,

and has no long-term health implications (Grieger, n.d.).

18. No Author

If no individual author of a web site document is indicated, cite either the name of an organization, group, or web site publisher or a shortened version of the title: (Cancer Care Ontario, 2000) or ("Reaching Out," 2000)

Better treatment and increased screening have likely contributed to falling breast

cancer death rates for women in Ontario (Cancer Care Ontario, 2000).

The program of training inmates as caregivers has been proposed to help with

integration ("Reaching Out," 2000).

19. Multiple Authors

Follow the same directions as those for citing multiple authors in books and periodicals (see pp. 27-28).

A recent major study conducted by the Psychology Department at the University of

Missouri-Columbia showed that real-life violent video game play increases aggres-

sive behaviour and delinquency (Anderson & Dill, 2000).

20. Entire Web Site

If an entire web site is being cited, and not a specific document from that web site, it is not necessary to include the site in the *References* list. The address of the site should be included in the text where the site is mentioned.

The web site for the Ministry of Health and Long Term Care offers a wealth of information about health care legislation as well as programs and services available in various communities throughout the province (http://www.gov.on.ca/health/index.html).

Other Publications

21. Comic Strip, Photograph, or Illustration

Cite the source of the comic strip, photograph, or illustration according to the correct format for that source: (Adams, 2002)

Dilbert characters reveal the power dynamics that exist within mentoring relationships (Adams, 2002).

Although best known for his abstracts, he ventures into realism in his most recent portraits of some of his painting peers (Rayner, 2001).

Note the *References* page entries in **Section 6**, pp. 54-55, for these examples.

22. Dictionary/Encyclopedia Definition

If the entry is unsigned (no author), use a shortened version of the title of the entry from the dictionary or encyclopedia in place of the author's name.

A fistula is defined as "an abnormal passage from an internal organ to the surface or between two internal organs" (*"Fistula,"* 1998, p. 637).

23. Personal Communication

Personal communication includes interviews, telephone conversations, letters, memos, and electronic communications (e.g., e-mail, discussion groups, messages from electronic bulletin boards). Give the initials as well as the surname of the communicator. Do not include personal communications in your *References* list.

As a registered massage therapist explained, "Therapeutic massage is an important part of our health care and is playing an ever-increasing role in the improvement of people's health" (K. Mackay, personal communication, October 18, 2002).

Note the use of initials as well as the surname in a personal communication citation.

"Life is a promise; fulfill it."

—Mother Theresa, 1910-1997

5

Preparing Your Reference List

Preparing Your Reference List

The last page of your research paper is the *References* list in which you list all of the sources cited within the text of your paper (except for personal communication).

Do not include materials consulted in your research that were *not* directly cited in your paper.

Building a Reference Entry

Think of each part of a reference entry as a unit. Each unit is separated by a period.

Book

Author.	(Date).	*Title.*	Location: Publisher.

Schoen, S. (2000). *The truth about fiction.* Upper Saddle River, NJ: Prentice Hall.

Periodical

Author.	(Date).	Title of article.	*Periodical Title, Volume* (issue), Page(s).

Bowman, K. (2000, October/November). The death penalty. *American Enterprise, 11* (7), 60-77.

Electronic Sources

Author.	(Date).	Title of article.	*Title of Periodical.*	Retrieval Statement

Avery, R. (2000, October 19). Official knew in '95 of E.coli in town's water. *The Toronto Star,* p. A4. Retrieved October 28, 2000, from http://www.thestar.com

Note that no period follows the retrieval statement except when referencing a database.

Reference entries for online sources follow the same pattern as print source entries. Each entry includes the following retrieval statement that provides the online source details:

Retrieved [date], from [URL]

Note on citing URLs

Cite only the URL from the search screen page, *not* the URL generated by a web site's internal search page. For example, you would cite the web site address for an article from *The Toronto Star* as

http://www.thestar.com

NOT

http://www.thestar.com/editorial/walkerton/20000102NEW04_INQUIRYS.html

If the URL address is for a deep link within a web site that can be accessed through this address, the entire address is to be used. For example, you would cite the URL for the article "Reaching Out to Help One Another" as follows:

Reaching out to help one another. (2000). *Let's Talk 25* (2). Retrieved October 26, 2000, from

http://www.csc-scc.gc.ca/text/pblct/letstalk/2000/vol2/1_e.shtml

Setting Up a Reference Page

List entries **alphabetically**

Italicize the titles of print, audiovisual, and online works (books, journals, newspapers, magazines, reports, web documents, brochures, films, videos, and television and radio productions)

Enclose non-routine information in **square brackets** immediately after the title and before the period

Do not use **"p." or "pp."** for articles in magazines or scholarly journals

Capitalize the first letter only of the title of an article

Italicize volume numbers and do not use "Vol." before the number

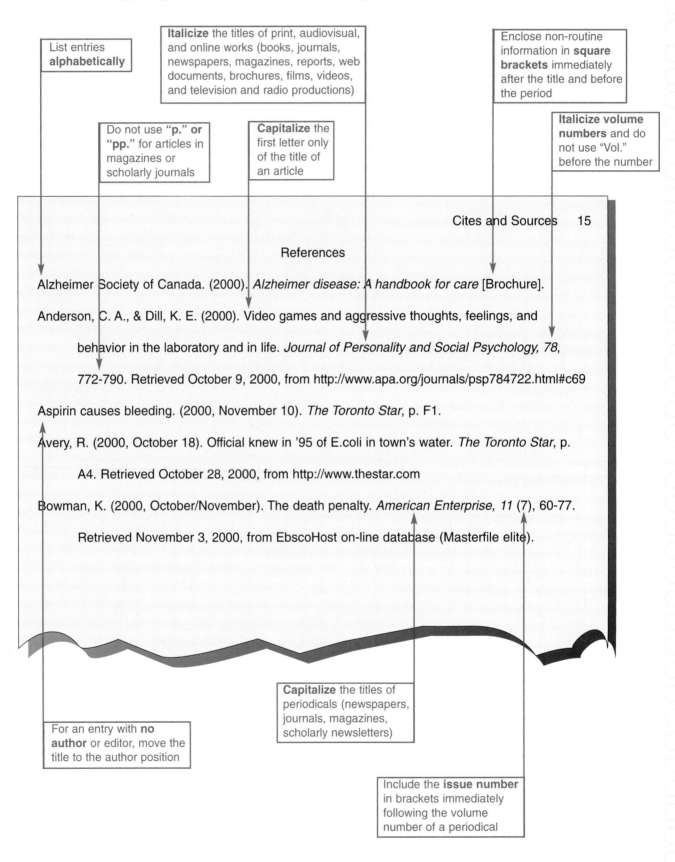

References

Alzheimer Society of Canada. (2000). *Alzheimer disease: A handbook for care* [Brochure].

Anderson, C. A., & Dill, K. E. (2000). Video games and aggressive thoughts, feelings, and

   behavior in the laboratory and in life. *Journal of Personality and Social Psychology, 78*,

   772-790. Retrieved October 9, 2000, from http://www.apa.org/journals/psp784722.html#c69

Aspirin causes bleeding. (2000, November 10). *The Toronto Star*, p. F1.

Avery, R. (2000, October 18). Official knew in '95 of E.coli in town's water. *The Toronto Star*, p.

   A4. Retrieved October 28, 2000, from http://www.thestar.com

Bowman, K. (2000, October/November). The death penalty. *American Enterprise, 11* (7), 60-77.

   Retrieved November 3, 2000, from EbscoHost on-line database (Masterfile elite).

For an entry with **no author** or editor, move the title to the author position

Capitalize the titles of periodicals (newspapers, journals, magazines, scholarly newsletters)

Include the **issue number** in brackets immediately following the volume number of a periodical

Set the first line of each entry flush left and indent subsequent lines

Write "(n.d.)" if there is **no date** of publication

Capitalize the first letter only of the title of a non-periodical (books, brochures, web documents, audio-visual productions)

Use **"p."** or **"pp."** for books, newspaper articles, and works in anthologies

Canadian Heritage Parks Canada. (n.d.). *Canada's national parks and national historic sites*

[Brochure].

Carey, E. (2001, February 2). Disabled adults still not part of community. *The Toronto Star*, p. A18.

Grossman, D., & DeGaetano, G. (1999). *Stop teaching our kids to kill: A call to action against TV,*

movie & video game violence. New York: Crown.

Holowaty, E. J., Marrett, L. D., Parkes, R., & Fehringer, G. (1998, October). *Colorectal cancer in*

Ontario 1971-1996: Incidence and mortality. Toronto, ON: Surveillance Unit of the Division of

Preventive Oncology Cancer Care Ontario. Retrieved October 10, 2000, from

http://www.cancercare.on.ca

Statistics Canada. *Online catalogue of products and services.* Retrieved November 1, 2000, from

http://www.statcan.ca/english/search/ips.html

For online sources, include the address for the **search screen** rather than the long URL generated by the search engine

Capitalize the first letter of a word that follows a colon

Use **"&"** to join the surnames of the last two authors

Include a **retrieval statement** for online sources

General Formatting Rules

Formatting reference list entries according to APA-style documentation rules requires close attention to detail. The following rules provide the general guidelines. For examples of the most common sources that writers and students use as references see **Section 6: Reference List Entries.**

Order of References

• Arrange entries alphabetically by surname of the first author:

Carey, E. (2001, February 2). Disabled adults still not part of community. *The Toronto Star*, p. A18.

Grossman, D., & DeGaetano, B. (1999). *Stop teaching our kids to kill: A call to action against TV, movie & video game violence.* New York: Crown.

• For an entry with no author or editor, move the title to the author position and list alphabetically by the first word of the title:

Aspirin causes bleeding. (2000, November 10). *The Toronto Star*, p. F1.

Avery, R. (2000, October 18). Official knew in '95 of E.coli in town's water. *The Toronto Star*, p. A4. Retrieved October 28, 2000, from http://www.thestar.com

• Arrange entries listed by title (no author) that begin with "The," "A," or "An," alphabetically according to the first letter of the word immediately following:

*The **D**oubleday Roget's thesaurus in dictionary form.*

*An **o**dyssey of Canadian verse.*

• Arrange multiple entries by the same author by year of publication, the earliest first:

Alder, B. **(1994).**

Alder, B. **(1998).**

• Arrange references by the same author with the same publication date alphabetically by title:

Frye, N. (1963). The **e**ducated imagination.

Frye, N. (1963). **F**ables of identity.

Frye, N. (1963). The **w**ell-tempered critic.

• Arrange references by different authors with the same surname alphabetically by the first initial:

Hamilton, **H.**

Hamilton, **J.**

• List group authors (associations, government agencies) alphabetically by the first word of the name:

Canadian Heritage Parks Canada.

Statistics Canada.

Capitalization

• Capitalize the first letter only of the title of an article or chapter:

Mastai, J. (2000, Winter). **Art on the street.** *Canadian Art, 17* (4), 61-66.

• Capitalize the first letter only of a non-periodical (books, brochures, web documents, audio-visual productions):

Canadian Heritage Parks Canada. (n.d.). ***Canada's national parks and national historic sites***

[Brochure].

• Capitalize the titles of periodicals (newspapers, journals, magazines, scholarly newsletters):

Mann, P. (2002, July 8). New vision urged for homeland security. ***Aviation Week & Space***

Technology, *157* (2), 40-41.

• Capitalize the first letter of a word that follows a colon:

Alzheimer Society of Canada, (2000). *Alzheimer disease*: *A handbook for care* [Brochure].

• Capitalize the first letter of each word of a title used in place of the author in an in-text citation:

Training inmates as caregivers was proposed to help with integration ("**Reaching Out,**" 2000).

- Capitalize the first letter of each word of the title of an entire work (book, film, periodical) when referred to in the text of your paper:

Many of these approaches are outlined in ***Alzheimer Disease: A Handbook for Care*** (Alzheimer Society of Canada, 2000).

- Capitalize the first letter of each word in the title of an article or chapter when referred to in the text of your paper:

Leslee Jaquette's article, **"Canadian Pacific Renews Environmental Initiative,"** outlines Phase Two of CP Hotel's corporate environmental program.

Using Italics

- Italicize the titles of print, audiovisual, and online works (books, journals, newspapers, magazines, reports, web documents, brochures, films, videos, and television and radio productions):

Meyers, D. (1998). ***Psychology*** (5th ed.). New York: Worth.

- Italicize the volume numbers of journals:

Irvin, S. (2002, Spring). No more boring art: A conceptual canon. *Canadian Art, 19* (1), 64-71.

- Italicize the titles of print, audiovisual, and online works (books, journals, newspapers, videos, etc.) when referred to in-text:

Canadian Pacific Hotels has also published ***The CPH & Green Partnership Guide*** (1992), a handbook offering practical advice to other hotels, institutions and restaurants on how to create an environmentally-friendly setting.

Using Brackets

- Use brackets (parentheses) to enclose the date of publication:

Bowman, K. **(2000, October/November).** The death penalty. *American Enterprise, 11* (7), 60-77.
Retrieved November 3, 2000, from EbscoHost on-line database (Masterfile elite).

• Use brackets to enclose the issue number (immediately following the volume number) of a periodical:

Bowman, K. (2000, October/November). The death penalty. *American Enterprise, 11* **(7)**, 60-77.

　　Retrieved November 3, 2000, from EbscoHost on-line database (Masterfile elite).

• Use square brackets immediately after the title and before the period to enclose non-routine information:

Canadian Heritage Parks Canada. (n.d.). *Canada's national parks and national historic sites*

　　[Brochure].

Pagination

• Use "p." or "pp." before the page numbers to reference articles or chapters in books, newspapers, and anthologies:

Carey, E. (2001, February 2). Disabled adults still not part of community. *The Toronto Star*,

　　p. A18.

Young, S. (1999). Polio was a killer – and Neil had it. In J. MacDonald (Ed.), *True north* **(pp. 53-**

　　59). Don Mills, ON: Addison-Wesley.

• Do not use "p." or "pp." to reference articles in magazines or scholarly journals:

Kirwin, R. (2002, Spring). Ancient harmonies. *Modern Painters*, **54-57.**

Date of Publication

• Give the date of publication in parentheses (brackets).
• For unpublished works, give the year the work was produced.
• For Internet sources, give either the date of publication or update or the date of retrieval.

- For newspapers, journals, magazines, and newsletters, use the following formats:

(2000, November 10).	[dailies and weeklies]
(1998, October).	[monthly journals, magazines, and newsletters]
(2000, October/November).	[bimonthly journals, magazines, and newsletters]
(2001, Spring).	[journals and magazines published quarterly or biannually]
(n.d.).	[work with no date available]
(in press).	[work accepted for publication but not yet printed]

Place of Publication and Publisher

- Include the place of publication for all nonperiodicals (books, brochures, web documents, audio-visual productions).

- Do not include the place of publication for periodicals (newspapers, journals, magazines, scholarly newsletters).

- List the place of publication as the city followed by the abbreviation for the state or province, and the name of the country if the publisher is outside North America. Use the Canada Post abbreviations for the names of provinces and states (e.g., ON for Ontario).

- The following locations can be listed without a state or country abbreviation because they are well-known for publishing: Baltimore, Boston, Chicago, Los Angeles, New York, Philadelphia, San Francisco; Amsterdam, Jerusalem, London, Milan, Moscow, Paris, Rome, Stockholm, Tokyo, and Vienna.

- Give the name of the publisher in as brief a form as possible. Omit terms such as *Publishers, Co.,* or *Inc.*

- When two or more publisher locations are given, give the location listed first in the book or, if specified, the location of the publisher's home office.

Other Elements of Style

• Use "&" to join the surnames of the last two authors or editors:

Anderson, C.A., **&** Dill, K.E. (2000). Video games and aggressive thoughts, feelings, and

behavior in the laboratory and in life. *Journal of Personality and Social Psychology, 78* (4),

772-790. Retrieved October 9, 2000, from http://www.apa.org/journals/psp/psp784722.html#c69

• Include a retrieval statement for online sources:

Bowman, K. (2000, October/November). The death penalty. *American Enterprise, 11* (7), 60-77.

Retrieved November 3, 2000, from EbscoHost online database (Masterfile elite).

• Include the address for the search screen rather than the long URL generated by the search engine for online sources:

Armstrong, J. (2002, July 23). US marijuana users seek Canadian haven. *The Globe and Mail,*

p. A1. Retrieved July 23, 2002, from **http://www.theglobeandmail.com**

"What is written without effort is, in general, read without pleasure."

–*Samuel Johnson, 1709-1784*

6

Reference List Entries

Reference
List Entries

The following list provides examples of the most common sources that writers and students use as references. The sample reference list items will show you in what order to present bibliographical information (author, date, title, publisher) and when to use italics, capitals, periods, spaces, etc., to format your entries.

For each type of reference entry (book, magazine, film, etc.), follow the format of the example exactly as printed. If you use a reference source not listed here, refer to the latest edition of the *Publication Manual of the American Psychological Association*.

You can also visit the APA web site at: http://www.apa.org/journals/webref.html. The site provides format suggestions and examples. APA also accepts e-mailed questions regarding citations.

Articles in Books or Periodicals

1. ARTICLE IN A MAGAZINE OR JOURNAL
2. ARTICLE IN A MAGAZINE OR JOURNAL (No Author)
3. ARTICLE IN A MAGAZINE OR JOURNAL (Volume and Issue)
4. ARTICLE IN A MAGAZINE OR JOURNAL (Special Issue)
5. ARTICLE IN A NEWSPAPER
6. ARTICLE IN A NEWSPAPER (No Author)
7. ARTICLE/CHAPTER IN AN EDITED BOOK OR ANTHOLOGY
8. ARTICLE/CHAPTER IN A MULTIVOLUME BOOK
9. EDITORIAL
10. EDITORIAL (No Author)
11. FOREWORD/PREFACE
12. INTRODUCTION IN A BOOK
13. LETTER TO THE EDITOR
14. REVIEW OF A BOOK/FILM/PERFORMANCE

Books and Brochures

15. BOOK BY ONE AUTHOR
16. BOOK BY TWO OR MORE AUTHORS
17. BOOK BY TRANSLATOR
18. BOOK IN MULTIPLE VOLUMES
19. BOOK IN REPUBLISHED EDITION
20. BOOK IN SECOND AND SUBSEQUENT EDITIONS
21. BOOK WITH AN AUTHOR AND EDITOR
22. BOOK/TEXTBOOK BY EDITOR
23. BROCHURE
24. BROCHURE (No Date)
25. CLASSICAL WORKS
26. GOVERNMENT DOCUMENT
27. GROUP OR CORPORATE AUTHORS

Electronic Sources

Other Publications

Articles in Books or Periodicals

1. Article in a Magazine or Journal

MacQueen, K. (2001, March 12). The best of both worlds: British Columbia aids the merger of traditional Chinese practice with western medicine. *Maclean's*, 44-47.

2. Article in a Magazine or Journal (No Author)

Reaching out to help one another. (2000). *Let's Talk*, *25* (2), 23-25.

3. Article in a Magazine or Journal (Volume and Issue)

Norris, G. (2002). Guided to land. *Flight International, 161* (4834), 34-35.

4. Article in a Magazine or Journal (Special Issue)

Jones, B.M. (2000). Multiculturalism and citizenship: The status of "visible minorities" in Canada [Special issue: Educating citizens for a pluralistic society]. *Canadian Ethnic Studies/Etudes Ethniques au Canada, 32,* 111-125.

Use square brackets to include non-routine information such as the title of a special issue or edition, as in the example above.

5. Article in a Newspaper

Aldrich, M. (2001, March 8). ASA may cut ovarian cancer. *The Globe and Mail*, p. A14.

6. Article in a Newspaper (No Author)

Aspirin causes bleeding. (2000, November 10). *The Toronto Star*, p. F1.

When no author is given, simply place the title in the author position.

7. Article/Chapter in an Edited Book or Anthology

Young, S. (1999). Polio was a killer – and Neil had it. In J. MacDonald (Ed.), *True north* (pp. 53-59). Don Mills, ON: Addison-Wesley.

8. Article/Chapter in a Multivolume Book

Berger, K.J., & Williams, M.B. (Eds.). (1999). Social, cultural, and spiritual aspects of health. In *Fundamentals of nursing: collaborating for optimal health* (2nd ed., Vol. 1, pp. 183-210). Stamford, CT: Appleton & Lange.

9. Editorial

Alang, N. (2002, May 9). To can a mockingbird [Editorial]. *The Globe and Mail*, p. A20.

10. Editorial (No Author)

Limits to collecting the DNA of criminals. (2002, May 13). [Editorial]. *The Globe and Mail*, p. A12.

When an editorial is unsigned (no author), begin the entry with the title of the editorial.

11. Foreword/Preface

Treat a Foreword, Preface, or Afterword as you would an Introduction (see item 12 in this list).

12. Introduction in a Book

Walton, B. (1999). Introduction. In J.R. Wooden, *Practical modern basketball* (3rd ed., pp. v-viii). Boston, MA: Allyn & Bacon.

13. Letter to the Editor

Stein, B. K. (1999, February 24). [Letter to the editor]. *New York Times* (National edition), p. 5:7.

14. Review of a Book/Film/Performance

Smith, S. (2002, May). Back in Bombay: Rohinton Mistry would like to write a novel about Canada. But India keeps getting in the way [Review of the book *Family matters*]. *Quill & Quire*, 14-15.

Books and Brochures

15. Book by One Author

Klein, N. (2000). *No logo: Taking aim at the brand bullies.* Toronto, ON: Random House.

16. Book by Two or More Authors

Rooke, C., & Rooke, L. (1998). *The writer's path: An introduction to short fiction.* Scarborough, ON: Nelson.

Balakrishnan, T.R., Lapierre-Adamcyk, E., & Krotki, K. J. (1993). *Family and childbearing in Canada: A demographic analysis.* Toronto: University of Toronto Press.

17. Book by Translator

Barskaya, A., Kantor-Gukovskaya, A., & Bessonova, M. (1995). *Paul Gauguin: Mysterious affinities* (A. Mikoyan, Trans.). Bournemouth, England: Parkstone/Aurora.

18. Book in Multiple Volumes

Berger, K.J., & Williams, M.B. (Eds.). (1999). *Fundamentals of nursing: Collaborating for optimal health* (2nd ed., Vol. 1). Stamford, CT: Appleton & Lange.

19. Book in Republished Edition

Ross, S. (2000). *As for me and my house.* Toronto, ON: McClelland & Stewart. (Original work published 1941)

20. Book in Second and Subsequent Editions

Guffey, M.E., & Nagle, B. (2000). *Essentials of business communication* (3rd Canadian ed.). Scarborough, ON: Nelson.

21. Book with an Author and Editor

Shelley, M. (2000). *Frankenstein* (2nd ed., J.M. Smith, Ed.). Boston: Bedford-St. Martin's. (Original work published 1818)

22. Book/Textbook by Editor

Barnet, S., Berman, M., Burto, W., Cain, W.E., & Stubbs, M. (Eds.). (2000). *Literature for composition: Essays, fiction, poetry, and drama* (5th ed.). New York: Longman.

23. Brochure

Research and Training Centre on Independent Living. (1993). *Guidelines for reporting and writing about people with disabilities* (4th ed.) [Brochure].

24. Brochure (No Date)

Canadian Heritage Parks Canada. (n.d.). *Canada's national parks and national historic sites* [Brochure].

25. Classical Works

You do not need to list major classical works, such as ancient Greek and Roman works and the Bible, in your *References* page. Refer to specific sections of classical works in the text of your paper by part (e.g., books, chapters, verses, lines, cantos). Identify the version you used in the first citation in your paper. For example: 1 Cor. 131:1 (Revised Standard Version).

26. Government Document

Statistics Canada. (1999). *Canadian Travel Survey* (87-212-XPB). Ottawa, ON: Ministry of Industry.

27. Group or Corporate Authors

Canadian Council of Ministers of the Environment. (1999). *Canadian environmental quality guidelines*. Winnipeg, MB: Author.

When the author is a group or corporation, the publisher is often the same organization. In this case, give the publisher's name as "Author."

Electronic Sources

28. Article from a Complex Web Site (Author Identified)

Holowaty, E.J., Marrett, L.D., Parkes, R., & Fehringer, G. (1998, October). *Colorectal cancer in Ontario 1971-1996: Incidence and mortality in Ontario*. Toronto, ON: Surveillance Unit of the Division of Preventative Oncology Cancer Care Ontario. Retrieved October 10, 2000, from http://www.cancercare.on.ca

29. Article from a Complex Web Site (No Author, No Date)

Attachment Disorder Network. (n.d.). *Parenting grandchildren*. Retrieved June 5, 2002, from http://www.radzebra.org/articles/grandchildren.htm

30. Article from a Magazine or Journal (Electronic Version)

Anderson, C.A., & Dill, K.E. (2000). Video games and aggressive thoughts, feelings, and behavior in the laboratory and in life. *Journal of Personality and Social Psychology, 78* (4), 772-790. Retrieved October 9, 2000, from http://www.apa.org/journals/psp/psp784722.html#c69

31. Article in an Internet-only Magazine or Journal (Author Identified)

Hamilton, H. (2000, October 26). Strength through diversity. *RCMP Online*. Retrieved October 30, 2000, http://www.rcmp-grc.gc.ca

32. Article in an Internet-only Magazine or Journal (No Author)

Reaching out to help one another. (2000). *Let's Talk 25* (2). Retrieved October 26, 2000, from http://www.csc-scc.gc.ca/text/pblct/letstalk/2000/vol2/1_e.shtml

33. Book by Corporate Author

Health Canada. (1998). *Canadian immunization guide* (5th ed.) [Online book]. Population
    and Public Health Branch. Retrieved October 23, 2000, from
    http://www.hc-sc.gc.ca/hpb/lcdc/publicat/immguide/index.html

34. Encyclopedia or Dictionary

Merriam-Webster Online. (2000). Retrieved April 6, 2001, from http://www.m-w.com

35. Entire Web Site

If an entire web site is being cited, and not a specific document from that web site, it is not
necessary to include the site in the *References* list. The address of the site should be
included in the text where the site is mentioned (see **Section 4: Using In-Text Citations,
item 20**).

36. Entry from an Encyclopedia or Dictionary (Author Identified)

Marsh, J. (2002). Inukshuk. In *The Canadian encyclopedia: Historica Foundation of
    Canada.* Retrieved May 13, 2002, from http://www.thecanadianencyclopedia.com

37. Entry from an Encyclopedia or Dictionary (No Author)

Phoenix. (2000). In *The Columbia electronic encyclopedia* (6th ed.). Retrieved October 2,
    2001, from http://www.encyclopedia.com/articles/10147.html

When no author is given, simply place the title of the entry in the author position.

38. Film or Video (Online)

Seattle skate for MS finish line flix: Finish time between 1:24:54 – 1:43:42 [Online video].
    (2000, September 22). Retrieved October 30, 2000, from http://wilsa.org/video/ssmsl.rm

39. Government Document

Industry Canada. (1999). Guides to Canadian industries. In *Strategis.* Retrieved November 1,
    2000, from http://strategis.ic.gc.ca/sc_indps/gci/engdoc/homepage.html

40. Government Document from CD-ROM Database

Statistics Canada. (1998). *Profile series* (Catalogue no. 95F0268XCB960000) [CD-ROM].

    Ottawa, ON: Author. Retrieved from Statistics Canada Census 96 database.

When the author is a group or corporation, the publisher is often the same organization. In this case, give the publisher's name as "Author."

41. Magazine or Journal Article from a Database

Bowman, K. (2000, October/November). The death penalty. *American Enterprise, 11* (7),

    60. Retrieved November 3, 2000, from EbscoHost online database (Masterfile elite).

42. News Release

Government of Canada. (2000, January 6). *Y2K monitoring and coordination centre*

    ceases operations [News release]. Retrieved October 28, 2000, from

    http://www.info2000.gc.ca

43. Newspaper Article

Fagan, D. (2000, October 9). Global fears raised over Israel. *The Globe and Mail.*

    Retrieved October 10, 2000, from http://www.globeandmail.com

44. Newspaper Article (No Author)

Families want 'friendly fire' inquiry reopened. (2002, July 22). *The Toronto Star.*

    Retrieved July 23, 2002, from http://www.thestar.com

45. Online Catalogue

Statistics Canada. *Online catalogue of products and services.* Retrieved November 1,

    2000, from http://www.statcan.ca/english/search/ips.html

46. Review of a Book/Film/Performance

Garcia, M. (n.d.). The fast runner (Atanarjuat) [Review of the motion picture *The Fast*

    Runner (Atanarjuat)]. *Film Journal International.* Retrieved June 7, 2002,

    from http://filmjournal.com/article.cfm/pageID/46199361

Other Publications

47. Comic Strip

Adams, S. (2002, June 15). Dilbert [Comic strip]. *The Toronto Star*, p. R1.

48. Encyclopedia/Dictionary

Porteus, A. (2000). *Dictionary of environmental science and technology*. Chichester, NY: J. Wiley.

Onions, C., et al. (Ed.). (1971). *The compact edition of the Oxford English dictionary* (Vols. 1-2). Glasgow, Scotland: Oxford University Press.

49. Entry in an Atlas

Bertruax, J.L. (1996). Comets. In J. Audouze & G. Israel (Eds.). *The Cambridge atlas of astronomy* (3rd ed., pp. 234-237). Cambridge: Cambridge University Press.

50. Entry in an Encyclopedia/Dictionary

Pratt, R. (1999). Phoenix. In *Encyclopedia of Greek mythology* (Vol. 3, pp. 521-522). Oxford: Oxford UP.

51. Entry in an Encyclopedia/Dictionary (No Author)

Fistula. (1998). *Mosby's medical, nursing, & allied health dictionary* (5th ed.). St. Louis, MO: Mosby.

When no author is given, simply place the title of the entry in the author position.

52. Film

Kunuk, Z. (Director). (2002). *The fast runner (Atanarjuat)* [Motion picture]. Canada: Lot 47 Films.

53. Music Recording

Lennon, J., & McCartney, P. (1965). In my life. On *Rubber soul* [Record]. London: Capitol.

54. News Release

Georgian College. (2001, March 8). *Women in Skilled Trades Program launched on International Women's Day* [News release].

55. Television Broadcast

Fry, M. (Executive Producer). (2001, March 10). *Committed* [Television broadcast]. Toronto, ON: CTV.

56. Unpublished Paper Presented in a Meeting

Rosch, J. (1995, June). *Transport Canada: Future with privatization*. Paper presented at Premier's Conference, Halifax, NS.

57. Video

Lam, M. (Director/Researcher), & Lynch, T., & Barrie, A.M. (Producers). (1998). *Show girls: Celebrating Montreal's legendary black jazz scene* [Video]. Canada: National Film Board of Canada.

58. Work of Art

Harris, L. S. (1917). *Snow* [Painting]. McMichael Canadian Art Collection, Kleinburg, Ontario.

Rayner, G. (2001). *Portrait of Emily Carr* [Painting]. Canadian Art 18 (4), 19.

Name the gallery or institution that houses the piece. If you refer to a photograph of a work, include the source of the reproduction in your entry, as in the second sample above.

"The highest result of education is tolerance."

–Helen Keller, 1880-1968

Model Reference List

Model Reference List

The following model lists sources referred to in this document. You can use this model to find out how particular source materials should be documented or as a checklist for your own *References* page.

Model   15

References

Alder, B. (1994). *Outwitting the neighbors.* New York: Putnam.

Aldrich, M. (2001, March 8). ASA may cut ovarian cancer. *The Globe and Mail,* p. A14.

Alzheimer Society of Canada. (2000). *Alzheimer disease: A handbook for care* [Brochure].

Anderson, C. A., & Dill, K. E. (2000). Video games and aggressive thoughts, feelings, and behavior in the laboratory and in life. *Journal of Personality and Social Psychology, 78* (4), 772-790. Retrieved October 9, 2000, from http://www.apa.org/journals/psp/psp784722.html#c69

Aspirin causes bleeding. (2000, November 10). *The Toronto Star,* p. F1.

Avery, R. (2000, October). Official knew in '95 of E.coli in town's water. *The Toronto Star,* p. A4. Retrieved October 28, 2000, from http://www.thestar.com

Bowman, K. (2000, October/November). The death penalty. *American Enterprise, 11* (7), 60-77. Retrieved November 3, 2000, from EbscoHost online database (Masterfile elite).

Canadian Council of Ministers of the Environment. (1999). *Canadian environmental quality guidelines.* Winnipeg, MB: Author.

Model   16

Canadian Heritage Parks Canada. (n.d.). *Canada's national parks and national historic sites* [Brochure].

Cancer Care Ontario. (2000, July). *Are breast cancer death rates increasing in Ontario?* Retrieved November 16, 2000, from http://www.cancercare.on.ca

Fagan, D. (2000, October 9). Global fears raised over Israel. *The Globe and Mail.* Retrieved October 10, 2000, from http://www.globeandmail.com

Fry, M. (Executive Producer). (2001, March 10). *Committed.* Toronto, ON: CTV.

Georgian College. (2001, March 8). *Women in Skilled Trades Program launched on International Women's Day* [News Release].

Government of Canada. (2000, January 6). *Y2K monitoring and coordination centre ceases operations* [News release]. Retrieved October 28, 2000, from http://www.info2000.gc.ca

Greening your travel experience. (1998, December). *USA Today Magazine, 127* (2643), 15.

Grieger, L. (n.d.). Are you a caffeine addict? Retrieved April 23, 2001, from http://www.ivillage.com/food/experts/nutrition/articles/0,5370,36692,00.html

Grossman, D., & DeGaetano, G. (1999). *Stop teaching our kids to kill: A call to action against TV, movie and video game violence.* New York: Crown.

Hamilton, H. (2000, October 26). Strength through diversity. *RCMP Online.* Retrieved October 30, 2000, from http://www.rcmp-grc.gc.ca

Health Canada. (1998). *Canadian immunization guide* (5th ed.) [Online book]. Population and Public Health Branch. Retrieved October 23, 2000, from http//www.hc-sc.gc.ca/hpb/lcdc/publicat/immguide/index.html

Heckman, G. (2000). *Nelson guide to Web research for Canadian students.*
Scarborough, ON: Nelson Thomson Learning.

Holland, R. (1999). Company's products purify air, water in hotel rooms. *Boston Business Journal, 19* (19), 9.

Holowaty, E. J., Marrett, L. D., Parkes, R., & Fehringer, G. (1998, October). Incidence and mortality. *Colorectal cancer in Ontario 1971-1996: Incidence and mortality.* Toronto, ON: Surveillance Unit of the Division of Preventive Oncology Cancer Care Ontario, 1-8. Retrieved October 10, 2000, from http://www.cancercare.on.ca/ocr/colorectal/incmort.pdf

Industry Canada. (1999). Guide to Canadian Industries. In *Strategis.* Retrieved November 1, 2000, from http://strategis.ic.gc.ca/sc_indps/gci/engdoc/homepage.html

Jaquette, L. (1998). Canadian Pacific renews environmental initiative. *Hotel & Motel Management, 213* (14), 32.

Jones, B. M. (2000). Multiculturalism and citizenship: The status of "visible minorities" in Canada [Special issue: Educating citizens for a pluralistic society]. *Canadian Ethnic Studies / Etudes Ethiques au Canada, 32,* 111-125.

MacQueen, K. (2001, March 12). The best of both worlds: British Columbia aids the merger of traditional Chinese practice with western medicine. *Maclean's,* 44-47.

Merriam-Webster Online. (2000). Retrieved April 6, 2001, from http://www.m-w.com

Myers, D. (1998). *Psychology* (5th ed.). New York: Worth.

Porteus, A. (2000). *Dictionary of environmental science and technology.* Chichester, NY: J. Wiley.

Model   18

Reaching out to help one another. (2000). *Let's Talk, 25* (2). Retrieved October 26, 2000, from http://www.csc-scc.gc.ca/text/pblct/letstalk/2000/vol2/1_e.shtml

Rosch, J. (1995, June). *Transport Canada: Future with privatization.* Paper presented at Premiers' Conference, Halifax, NS.

Seattle skate for MS finish line flix: Finish time between 1:24:54 – 1:43:42 [online video]. (2000, September 22). Retrieved October 30, 2000, from http://wilsa.org/video/ssmsl.rm

Statistics Canada. (1992). *Census divisions and census subdivisions: Reference maps* (92-319). Ottawa, ON: Department of Industry, Science and Technology.

Statistics Canada. (1998). *Profile series* (Catalogue no. 95F0268XCB96000) [CD-ROM]. Ottawa, ON: Author. Retrieved May 5, 2002, from Statistics Canada Census 96 database.

Statistics Canada. (1999). *Canadian Travel Survey* (87212-XPB). Ottawa, ON: Ministry of Industry.

Statistics Canada. *Online catalogue of products and services.* Retrieved November 1, 2000, from http://www.statcan.ca/english/search/ips.html

Troyer, W. (1992). *The CPH & R green partnership guide: 12 steps to help create an environmentally friendly setting for our guests, ourselves and our future.* Canada: Canadian Pacific Hotels & Resorts.

Vidatron Television (Producer). (1998). *Harm's way* [Video]. (Available from Kineticvideo.com, Toronto, ON)

Wagner, T. (1998). *Dealing with conflict.* Orville, NB: Sprite.

Young, S. (1999). Polio was a killer – and Neil had it. In J. MacDonald (Ed.), *True north* (pp. 53-59). Don Mills, ON: Addison-Wesley.

Zones, J. S. (2000). Beauty myths and realities and their impact on women's health. In M. B. Zinn, P. Hondagneu-Stelo, & M. A. Messner (Eds.), *Gender through the prism of difference* (2nd ed., pp. 87-103). Toronto, ON: Allyn & Bacon.

Notes

"Life is what happens to you when you are making other plans."

–John Lennon, 1940-1980

Index

index

Index

Additional Information

For additional information, consult the following manual, available in libraries:

American Psychological Association. (2001). *Publication manual of the American Psychological Association.*
(5th ed.). Washington, DC: American Psychological Association.

APA Web Site
You can also visit the APA web site, which provides format suggestions and examples at http://www.apa.org/
journals/webref.html.

APA also accepts e-mailed questions regarding citations.